FINANCIAL PLANNING WITH A BIBLICAL VIEW

MAURICE C. SMITH

WESTBOW
PRESS®
A DIVISION OF THOMAS NELSON
& ZONDERVAN

WestBow Press books may be ordered through booksellers or by contacting:

WestBow Press
A Division of Thomas Nelson & Zondervan
1663 Liberty Drive
Bloomington, IN 47403
www.westbowpress.com
1 (866) 928-1240

ISBN: 978-1-9736-9596-7 (sc)
ISBN: 978-1-9736-9597-4 (e)

Print information available on the last page.

WestBow Press rev. date: 08/03/2020

CONTENTS

REVIEWS

THIS BOOK IS DEDICATED
TO MY TWO FATHERS

I thank my heavenly Father Who, through His Word, has taught me to have the proper perspective of money. He extended His mercy and grace to me while I was learning His principle of "Sowing and Reaping."

I am also forever grateful to my earthly father Eugene, who passed away on December 13, 2017. He modeled the importance of financial responsibility before me – he understood the importance of saving and staying free of indebtedness. He once told my oldest sister, "It's okay to have money, but make sure money doesn't have you!"

A special thanks to Dr. Donald Nurse who has been an invaluable resource for the editing and formatting of this book.

PREFACE

The reader is advised that the author makes no claim or assertion of being an expert or licensed financial advisor. All suggestions are based on his personal opinions and experiences. It is the author's intent to give a Biblical viewpoint of finances, while presenting some practical guidelines as well. Different concepts and strategies are shared in order to give the reader alternate options. The testimonials are factual. However, the corresponding names were omitted in order to protect the privacy of the individuals. It is my sincere hope that this book will be a blessings and a lasting resource to all who read it.

Chapter 1

TITHING

The Background.

The principle of tithing is one of the most debated subjects in the Church today. Those who oppose tithing as a requirement argue that *New Testament Believers are not under the Laws of Moses, therefore, tithing does not apply to them.* This reasoning sounds legitimate until the facts are examined.

A Historical Perspective.

Let us begin with the fact that tithing existed before the Laws of Moses. For example, in the Book of Genesis, chapter 14 and verses 18 through 20 (KJV), it is noted that Abraham gave a tenth of his wealth to Melchizedek, known as the King of Salem, and Priest of the Most High (believed by many to be the pre-incarnate Christ). Secondly, it is interesting to note that the core principles of the Laws of Moses (the Ten Commandments), were not abolished – New Testament Believers are still forbidden to *lie, steal, murder, covet, commit adultery, and idolatry.* Romans 6:1 (KJV) reminds us that the Grace of God is not a license to continue in sin. I am not saying that those who do not tithe are sinning, but I am rather suggesting that they are utilizing the concept of Grace as an excuse and therefore conceal a deeper problem.

A third observation is that the tithe was instituted by God to meet the needs of His House (the Church). In Malachi 3:6 (KJV), God reminded the people that the God of the past was the same God of the present. He clearly pointed out that they had turned away from His Laws, and needed to return to Him. The people responded, *"In what way shall we return?"(Malachi 3:7, NKJV)* God's response to their question highlights the essence of this discussion, He said, *"Will a man rob God?"(Malachi 3:8 NKJV).* They were so oblivious of their transgression that they had to probe further with another query, *"In what way have we robbed*

You?"(Malachi 3:8, NKJV). God's reply indicated that they were robbing Him by neglecting to tithe and to give offerings. He further commanded them to bring the full tithe to His House (the Church), so that it would lack nothing. In addition, He promised that if His people would give faithfully, then He would release a *return* that was greater than their *investment!*

Providing for the Church.

Imagine, if businesses did not have prices for their goods and services, but left it up to their customers to pay whatever they felt like paying! How long do you believe such businesses would last? The Church, although not a secular business entity, is not exempt from this principle – it has operating expenses as well. God clearly stated that those who withhold the tithe are robbing Him. Some people when they are faced with that truth may feel guilty. However, in many instances their response is, *"I would like to tithe but I can't afford to do so."* That sounds like a valid reason not to tithe, that is, until one considers Luke 21:1 – 4 (NKJV); it speaks of the widow who gave her last mite as an offering!

The Law of Reciprocity.

Consider the widow in 1 Kings 17:10-14 (NKJV) who was asked by the prophet Elijah to give him her last meal during a time of famine. This would appear to be an unreasonable request in the circumstances except, the widow received God's guarantee from the prophet, that should she obey and gave what she had, God would always meet her needs. The widow heard God's promise, she believed God's promise, she trusted God's promise, and she received God's promise. Luke 6:38 (NKJV) says, "Give, and it will be given to you, good measure, pressed down, shaken together, and running over, will be put into your bosom. For with the measure you use, it will be measured back to you." This is the Kingdom principle Jesus taught! So, why do Christians pray for abundance while giving God less than the required minimum – the tithe? The answer is simple, many Christians do not truly believe God's principle of *Sowing and Reaping* – others believe but do not obey. If you do not obey God, you cannot receive His promises! Further, if you do not receive His promises you cannot learn to trust Him.

An Issue of Trust.

The root cause of opposition to tithing is trust. Unfortunately, we have more trust in man's financial system than in God's promises for our provision. The same people for example, who say they can't afford to tithe, will book an expensive cruise well in advance – and without any money at the time, but rather believing that the money would be available when it was actually required. Also, these individuals will use a credit card to purchase things they can not afford, believing that they would subsequently be able to pay off the credit card debt. They seem to exercise faith only when they are the recipients.

A Question of Ownership.

There is another issue that impacts this situation. These Believers who are unwilling to tithe, fail to understand that their money and possessions do not belong to them! The parable of the unjust steward lets us know that we are merely managers of God's money. The Scriptures declare, *"It is He who gives you power to get wealth ...."* (Deuteronomy 8:18, NKJV). Jesus, when asked about paying taxes responded by advising that what belonged to Caesar should be given to Caesar, and what belonged to God should be given to God – the tithe belongs to God. Until one settles the question of ownership, there will always be a struggle with tithing!

The Genius of Percentages.

I recall struggling with tithing thirty years ago. When I think about it now, I just can't figure why I made such a big deal about it then! The genius of the tithe is, it does not matter how little or how much one makes - the percentage calculations ensure that each contribution is proportionate. For example, if someone makes $100,000 per year, the tithe (10%), on that amount is $10,000. Similarly, the tithe on $50,000 earned per year would be $5,000. Likewise, an annual wage of $25,000 would yield a tithe of $2,500. In each instance the corresponding amount due as a tithe is relatively equal to the other since each is equivalent to 10% of the amount earned. People at the $25,000 range would often say, "If I were making $50,000, I would tithe." And, the people at the $50,000 range would say, "If I were making $100,000, I would tithe." The truth of the matter is, if one refuses to tithe at the lower level of income, it is unlikely and perhaps even doubtful that that individual would tithe even if the income was doubled.

Faithful Stewardship.

Jesus taught in Matthew 25:14-30 (NKJV) that individuals who were unfaithful with little would be unfaithful with much. He illustrated this tendency in the parable of the talents. This story begins with a man who was going on a journey. He entrusted his money to three of his servants before he left. He gave one servant five (5) talents, to another he entrusted two (2), and finally one (1) talent to another servant. They were not only expected to manage his money, but see to it that he got a return. When the man returned from his journey, he sought an account from those to whom he had entrusted his funds. The servant who was given five (5) talents, doubled the money entrusted to him, and so likewise did the servant who was given two (2) talents. However, the servant who was given one (1) talent had no increase to present to his master. All he really had to do was to gain one (1) other talent – that would have doubled what he was originally given. The truth is that he was lazy, and did not care for his master's well-being. His attitude caused him to lose the trust of his master, who promptly took away the talent and gave it instead to that faithful servant who had doubled the five (5) talents entrusted to him. The latter now had eleven (11) talents.

Tithing is also an indicator of the condition of one's heart. Jesus on one occasion stated that where you place your treasures, that's where your heart is. There are people who would spend over $1,000 for an iPhone, but would never give that much to their Church if asked. The Bible explains the futility of investing in earthly things when compared to investing in things of the Kingdom. It also clearly states that we cannot serve two masters – we are going to serve either God or money! If you are struggling to release the tithe, it simply means that money has a grip on you. You will become a recipient of God's promises once you decide to tithe and to trust God. Then, among other things, you will experience the power, purpose, and pleasure of giving!

Honoring God First.

I shared the contents of this book prior to it being published, and I was asked why I chose the subject of Tithing as the first chapter. My response was, *"Because it represents our firstfruits. It also demonstrates where our priorities lie."* Before we entertain any financial consideration towards anyone or anything, we must first honor God. Regretfully, too many Christians place the Lord at the bottom of their financial list. Consequently He receives their leftovers instead of their best.

The Right Attitude.

Some Believers vow that as soon as their money situation improved, that they would begin to tithe. I am not an advocate of conditional giving! If you only tithe when conditions are favorable, then you would be giving from a position of convenience and not faith. The Book of 2 Samuel 24:24 teaches us the proper attitude toward giving; David declined a generous offer from Araunah. The latter desired to give David the oxen for sacrifice, and the material to build the altar for that sacrifice to God. However, David's response was, "No, but I will surely buy it from you for a price; nor will I offer burnt offerings to the Lord my God with that which costs me nothing." (2 Samuel 24:24, NKJV).

Failure to put tithing first when it comes to your financial planning is like putting the cart before the horse. If you do not operate under God's principles, how can you receive His blessings!

CHAPTER 2

ELIMINATE DEBT

The Issue of Debt.

The Bible declares that the borrower is slave to the lender. It also declares that God intended that His people would be at the head of things and not at the tail. There is no difference between Believers and non-Believers when it comes to debt! According to the U. S. Census Bureau, the average household now has a debt of $137,000 – this includes credit cards, car notes, and mortgage balances. You will never experience financial freedom until you solve the debt issue! Some people equate making a lot of money with financial freedom. But, there are some millionaires who are financially in a worst position than individuals with far less income.

The Root Cause of Debt.

Contrary to public opinion, it does not matter how much money one has coming in – it matters more how much is going out! The true problem is not a lack of money, but rather debt. In order to eliminate debt, the root cause must be ascertained. Many Christians will deny it however, but their debt is rooted in covetousness. The reason for this opinion is based on the observation that most purchases are motivated as a result of advertisements. This multi-billion dollar industry of advertisement has manipulated the American public to the point that individuals believe that they cannot live without a particular product or service – advertisement serves as the motivating factor for their purchases.

Advertisment and F.O.M.O.

A great example is seen when a new generation of the iphone is placed on the market – people with perfectly good phones feel that they must have the latest and greatest model. The culture has an acronym for this condition called F.O.M.O. It stands for, *'Fear Of Missing Out.'* Businesses know this, that is why they will spend millions of dollars for a two minute Superbowl AD. Advertisement is so powerful that in the early sixties, certain advertising techniques were prohibited. For example, movie theatres were inserting images of foaming Coca-Cola and popcorn at the bottom of the screen while the movie was playing – this sublimely caused people to be hungry and thirsty!

Images and Social Status.

Most commercials are designed to cause you discontentment in various areas of your life – where you live, what you drive, and what brand of clothing you wear. This creates an atmosphere of covetousness. Most people are content with what they have, that is, until they see an advertisement representing a product which appears to have a greater social status than their current version. We live in a society where image and perception are very important. Unfortunately, many Christians are more concerned with how they are perceived by others, rather than with how God sees them. Luke 12:15 (NKJV) records the words of Jesus addressing this issue. He said, "Take heed and beware of covetousness, for one's life does not consist in the abundance of the things he possesses." In other words, your net worth does not determine your self-worth! Once you embrace that truth you will begin to move in the right direction – you will no longer buy things to impress others – you will no longer try to keep up with the Jones – you will no longer determine your self – worth based on where you live, what you drive or what you wear!

Some Considerations Before Spending.

The first step toward eliminating debt is to bring your spending under control. I have learned to ask myself three important questions before making any significant purchase: 1. Why am I buying it? 2. Can I do without it? 3. Can I afford it? I still have to justify the cost, even if the purchase gets the green light. For example, I may need to buy a car because I need transportation. However, I must now decide between the car I *want*, and the car I *need*. The car I want costs $60,000, its reliability is above average, but its maintenance, insurance premiums, and monthly payments are all high. Conversely, the car I need costs $30,000, its reliability is good, its maintenance and insurance costs are average, while the monthly payments are low. It should be obvious which purchase makes the most financial sense when both options are compared, even if you could afford either. We make the wrong choices too many times based on superficial reasons.

A Wise Approach.

When you make wise decisions with your income, you will reduce the amount of funds going out. Many people live from paycheck to paycheck without assessing their actual financial condition. You need to know exactly what your expenses are in order to get out of debt. You need to begin by listing the value of all your monthly expenses:

EXPENSES:	COSTS:
Mortgage/Rent	$
Car Note	$
Gas	$
EXPENSES CONTD	**COSTS**
Repairs	$
Taxes	$
Food	$

Utilities	$
Cell Phone	$
T.V.	$
Internet	$
Insurance (auto, Home, Life)	$
Credit Cards	$

Once you total your monthly expenses, subtract the amount from your monthly net income – reality will set in! The average person will discover that they are spending far more than they are making – that, is a recipe for disaster.

A Sensible Assessment and Action.

Now you must decide to take action in order to reduce your expenses. First, eliminate all non-essential expenses such as that gym membership which you have never used. Next, you need to do a cost analysis of each essential bill. I have no allegiance to any company. So, when I found a car insurance that offered a $1,000 discount per year for the same coverage I currently had, I immediately switched companies. I have reduced my bills 20-40% by doing this routinely with all of them.

Decreasing your bills will increase the amount of money you have at your disposal. Instead of looking at this as extra money available for the purchase of more things, see it as an opportunity to pay off the biggest debt trap, credit cards. It is vital that you have a plan to eliminate credit card debt.

Planning The Debt Elimination Strategy.

A wise man once said, "A failure to plan is a plan to fail." Start with the card that carries the lowest balance. The moment that account is paid in full, you will feel empowered. This will free up money to pay off the next credit card. If you need motivation to continue, consider this – it's the credit card company's goal to keep you in debt as long as possible. Here's why, if you make the minimum monthly payment of $150 on a credit card with a balance of $7,000 @18%, it will cost you $12,129.00 over a period of 6.75 years to complete the total payments.

The Cost of Debt.

Most people become angry when they learn that someone has taken advantage of them, yet they accept these excessive interest rates charged by these companies. Every time that I am tempted to use a credit card, I remind myself of the cost! I believe that a debit card is a great alternative because you are spending your own money, and are limited to what you could afford. We will discuss this further under the section dealing with saving.

It would be a good idea to retain just one major credit card after you have eliminated your credit card debt. Place the others in a secure place, or cut them up if the temptation to use them is too strong. Nevertheless, do not close the accounts – doing so will adversely affect your credit score since you would be diminishing the amount of funds available for credit use. Once you have learned to minimize your expenses and eliminate your debt, now you are in position to determine your financial future. More importantly, you have relieved yourself from the stress and burden so many people live under. You must understand that it will take patience and perseverance to accomplish your goals. It may take more time than anticipated, but it will be worth the wait!

>> CHAPTER 3 <<

SAVING

<u>Faith and Responsibility.</u>

Some Christians have a misconception about saving. They believe that that their lack of planning and saving is a sign of faith. This is nothing but presumption in their interpretation of the Scriptures! When Jesus said in Matthew 6:25 (NKJV paraphrase), "Do not be anxious about what you should eat, drink, or what you will wear ..." – His promise to provide our needs did not mean that there was no responsibility on our part. Every Believer might as well quit his or her job if that were so. The verse is really saying that we should not be consumed with worry concerning those things!

Planning and Saving.

The Bible gives us a picture of the importance of planning and saving. We know that Joseph's trials and tribulations were all a part of God's master plan. God took him from the pit to the palace in order that he may serve God's purpose. He gave Joseph the ability to foresee the future, and the wisdom to plan accordingly. When Joseph interpreted Pharaoh's dream, he revealed that there would be seven years of abundance followed by seven years of severe famine. Joseph exercised wisdom by ordering one fifth of all produce to be stored during the time of plenty. They stored food and grain. So, when the famine came, they had reserves which God, through Joseph, had prepared for Jacob and his family – Joseph's kin. The lesson learned from this Biblical account is that one does not wait for an emergency before preparing for it. Often, in times of abundance we live our lives as if there is no tomorrow. If there's one thing that history has taught us is that it's not a matter of whether we will face an emergency, but rather when!

The Imperative of Saving.

It is reported by those who conduct statistical analysis that 50% of Americans do not possess enough savings to handle an emergency over $500. Even if the percentage of error is 10%, it still represents an alarming number of people who are one emergency away from despair. If you never understood the importance of saving, the Pandemic of 2020 has taught us that one's financial situation can change overnight. My father tried to teach me at an early age that for every dollar earned, I needed to put a little away for *a rainy day.* He grew up poor, and lived through the Great Depression. Consequently, he never took present provisions for granted.

A Dedicated Saving Account.

It is essential that once you reduce your expenses and eliminate debts, that you should create a *Dedicated Emergency Savings Account.* Most jobs allow for allotments to be taken from your income, and to be directly deposited into an account of your choice. I have found that this is the most painless, yet efficient way to save. You would be pleasantly surprised at the speed with which your savings account would grow with an allotment of 10% from your income. Remember, it's an emergency fund, a new iPhone is not considered an emergency.

Some Considerations.

Most financial advisors recommend that you endeavor to retain savings that would cover about six months of usual expenses. I would suggest that you never combine your savings with your checking account. In order to avoid dipping into your emergency account, you should establish a *Mad Money Account* with a debit card. This allows you to pay for non-emergencies such as eating out, entertainment, and all miscellaneous expenses without impacting your emergency fund. Once you build up your emergency fund, forget about it – treat it as though it does not exist. If you experience and expend funds on a real emergency such as a busted hot water heater, or a broken down car, then ensure that you continue to save until the money utilized is replaced. Despite the fact that it's really your own money, you must treat the used funds as a loan. The lack of an emergency savings account is a major contributor to credit card debt.

Saving for Retirement.

Saving for your retirement is critical – failure to do so will result in a financially challenging retirement. Take my word for it – no matter how young you are, that time will come sooner than you think. The sooner you begin saving, the better off you will be when the time for retirement comes. This is so because at that time it is likely that your income would be significantly reduced. Your savings or lack thereof will determine your quality of life.

Recognizing Opportunities to Save.

I remember having a conversation with a 40 year old co-worker two years prior to my own retirement. He had been employed for about 12 years, but never bothered to enroll in the 401K plan available through our employer. I explained to him that he was passing up a great opportunity. He was not taking advantage of the ability to save up to 10% tax deferred, with the company matching up to 5% at a rate of 3% dollar for dollar, and the remaining 2% at 50 cents for each dollar. He thanked me for my concern after I was through, but was still not interested. Let us examine a hypothetical situation relative to his condition to give you an idea of the kind of money he was leaving on the table. If he started to contribute to the 401K plan at age forty, then 5% of his pay for 25 years with an 8% average rate of return would have yielded him approximately $365,935.00 at age 65. I don't think that he really understood that our retirement system was based on three sources of income, our pension, Social Security, and our 401K plan. He was left with only two streams of income by forfeiting the 401k plan. Imagine attempting to sit on a three-legged stool that had one leg missing! If he lives to retire, he's going to live to regret foregoing the opportunity to save through the 401K plan. He's going to discover what all retired individuals know – if you don't have sufficient funds saved, your financial options will be very limited.

Considering an IRA.

The benefit of having an IRA (Individual Retirement Account) is seen in the fact that after age 59 ½ one can make withdrawals to supplement one's income. You would also have the opportunity to convert it to an annuity or self-directed IRA that allows investment in Real Estate, Tax Liens, Gold and

Silver etc. If you have a choice between a Traditional IRA and a Roth IRA, you should know that it is the Roth IRA that gives you the best advantage and flexibility.

Chapter 4

FINANCIAL EDUCATION

The Power of Knowledge.

Hosea 4:6 (NKJV) reads, *"My people are destroyed for lack of knowledge, because you have rejected knowledge."* Here, God condemns His people because they had no desire to know Him or His ways. This led to their demise. Likewise, many Christians have no desire to gain financial knowledge. Whoever coined the phrase, "What you don't know can't hurt you," never considered the consequences of ignorance – financial ignorance can cost you thousands of dollars!

Knowledge and Money Management.

I recall listening to cassettes about money management 40 years ago. That time was well spent – it taught me that 20-30% of any income I earned would likely be taxable. The information I gleaned over those years also taught me how I could legally reduce or eliminate my tax liability. This knowledge has served to save me thousands of dollars over the years. I have learned that *how much you make is less important than how much you keep*!

Knowledge and Credit Ratings.

A converse observation to the preceding paragraph is that my ignorance of credit ratings caused me to lose thousands of dollars. It was not until 5 years ago that I began to read about how credit scores are calculated, and why they matter. I found out that Credit Bureaus monitor all of our financial transactions – they record our late payments, non-payments, liens, bankruptcies, and our *Income to Debt Ratio*. Needless to say that any negative reports in your portfolio would serve to lower your credit score – the lower your score, the higher the interest rate you are charged to do business. That does not sound like a big deal until you crunch the numbers.

Let us compare two people with different credit scores applying for a $200,000 mortgage with a duration of 30 years. The person with an excellent credit rating will be charged 3.5% with $898 as the monthly payment. This means that person will pay $85,655 in total interest. The person with a fair credit rating will be charged 6% for a similar transaction, and will have to pay $1,199 per month. That person will end up paying $151,875 in total interest. The difference of 2.5 percentage points will cost or save you $66,220.

It is important that you request a free annual report each year. This will help you to discern any erroneous information on your credit report that you were not privy to – this may have been costing you thousands of dollars. You have the right to challenge any false information on your report.

Do Your Own Calculations.

I am reminded of another reason why people are paying high interest rates. The early 2000s was the height of the housing boom – a time when homes were going up in value, while lending rates were going down. Thousands of people were refinancing their mortgages at lower interest rates - saving themselves thousands of dollars. I discovered that many people were obtaining rates lower that 5%, while I was still paying a whopping 9% since the 90s.

Banks began to solicit home owners who had a lot of equity in their properties. I was receiving at least one phone call per day from mortgage companies. At first, I welcomed the opportunity to improve my financial situation. However, time after time they would begin by promising that they could lower my payments significantly. But, after making their calculations, the best proposal anyone could come up with was to lower my current interest by 1.5%. The related facts became an education for me. For example if I accepted such a proposal, I would need to pay (1) Points, (2) Originating Fees, (3) Closing Costs. When I considered everything, I discovered that the Mortgage Companies were the only ones benefitting from the refinancing!

It's Your Call.

I was so frustrated with all of this that one day I answered the phone prepared to go on the offensive with the mortgage lender. I opened the conversation by saying to him, "Before you start promising me anything, unless you can offer me 5%, no points, no origination fees, no closing costs, and a fixed rate, then don't waste my time or yours." Needless to say, the conversation was over. After I hung up, I went to my room, got on my knees, and brought my complaint before the Lord. When I got up ten minutes later, I had this unction to call my mortgage company. At first, I dismissed it as a crazy thought. I found myself addressing the issue as many Christians do – we ask God for a solution to our problem, but because it does not seem to make sense, we doubt the source. However, the thought persisted, and so I decided to call my mortgage company. I asked them why the rate offered to me was so high while others I knew were obtaining lower rates. The person responded by saying, *"Mr. Smith, we do have refinancing that we can offer you with no points, no origination fees, no closing costs, and a 5% fixed rate."* The Bible says, *"...You do not have because you do not ask."* (James 4:2, NKJV).

Seeking Financial Education.

Your credit score not only determines your interest rate, but also whether or not you would be approved for a loan. Most people do not realize that their credit score is used by insurance companies for premium rates, businesses do the same for employment, and landlords for tenant evaluation. This revelation created a hunger in me for relevant financial information. I began to read financial magazines and books, to attend free and paid seminars, and to view Specials on Public Television. I never earned an academic degree, but instead acquired valuable knowledge and experience.

Choosing Mentors.

Another critical aspect of your financial education is to seek a mentor who has already attained what you are trying to accomplish. I learned to address a simple question in multi-level marketing, *"Why do poor people take advice from other poor people?"* This was not meant to demean poor people, but was rather referring to the prevalence of ill advice that most financially challenged people are likely to give to others.

A well-known author wrote about two people who mentored him while growing up. He wanted to know at a very young age how to create wealth. One mentor was a highly educated professor who, however, was just getting by financially. In comparison, the other mentor with an eighth grade level of education had multiple streams of income and a net worth of millions. Who do you think he modeled himself after? We saw this displayed when the greatest basketball player since Michael Jordan sought out the richest man in the world to mentor him after he signed a multimillion dollar contract. A good mentor can help you avoid the pitfalls, and show you how to navigate around obstacles.

Assets vs. Liabilities.

One of the most underrated and misunderstood financial principles is that of Assets vs. Liabilities. Once again I quote a lesson learned from training in multi-level marketing. The instructors frequently challenged people's objection to spending a few hundred dollars for additional training by asking this question, *"How much money is that flat screen T.V. you bought making you?"* The obvious point is that we have no problem investing money in things that have no return value, yet we are often reluctant to invest in things that can result in a return. Understanding the difference between an *asset* and a *liability* will drastically change your spending and investing habits.

Thirty years ago, if given the choice between a

brand new luxury car and a fixer up rental property for the same price, I would have probably chosen the car. Fortunately, I now have the advantage of knowing that in less than 5 years the car's value would depreciate – it will be worth 50% less and would have cost me significantly in repairs and insurance. While on the other hand, the rental property would cost me initially, but would appreciate in value – more importantly, when compared with the car, the rental property would continue to generate income well beyond the usefulness of the former. Simply put, liabilities will take money from you, while assets will put money into your pocket.

Retirement Plans.

Planning for retirement should be another aspect of your financial education. This should include IRAs, 401Ks, and other retirement plans. If you have a plan, you should understand your options, restrictions, and rights. I am amazed at how so many people believe the stock market is too complicated, and consequently make no decisions concerning their accounts. Some people believe that the broker is going to protect their assets against losses. However, no matter how honest the broker may be, no one cares about your money more than you do! Last year I gave some sound financial advice to someone who was concerned about outliving her IRA. She, however, was not persistent enough with her broker who neglected to follow through with my advice. A year later the market crashed and she was complaining about the hit she took – I had no comment! Financial fear is a two edged sword. Many people are afraid to use a different strategy because they think they will lose money. Instead, they do nothing, and continue to lose money.

A little known strategy called a self directed IRA gives you unbelievable advantage and the ability to invest in safe assets. I will give more details and reasons in the Building Wealth chapter concerning why you need to understand this strategy.

Life Insurance.

Your financial portfolio should also include a life insurance policy. When I was twenty five years of age, I had this foolish notion that life insurance was just for old people. Like so many presumptuous young people, I assumed that I would not die at a young age. Aside from being foolish, I was selfish because I was not considering the welfare of my family – I was not thinking of their financial well-being should

I be deceased. I admit that learning about insurance policies is not the most exciting subject. However, it is more important than you may realize. You need adequate Insurance, and the right kind – the amount will depend on your financial condition.

Choosing The Right Policy.

There are over a dozen kinds of Insurance Policies. Most agents will try to sell you a Whole Life or Universal Live policy. The truth is, all you really need is Term Life Insurance because it costs far less for the same amount of Insurance coverage. The other reason is that the older you become, the less Insurance you should need, and Term Life gives you that flexibility. The more costly Whole Life Policy is an Invest/Insurance Plan. This is a bad idea because the R.O.I (Return on Investment) is very low. Smart investors never invest through a Life Insurance Policy. Many have unknowingly thrown away thousands of dollars going down that road. Advantage is taken over those individuals who never take the time to learn about what they are buying.

I was introduced to the Insurance world over thirty years ago when I joined a Multi-Level Marketing Company – it was licensed to sell Insurance and

Securities. Their philosophy was, *"Buy Term & invest the rest."* After seeing the calculations between the two strategies, I was convinced of what they were saying. One of my favorite quotes is, *"Liars figure, but figures don't lie!"*

What About Inflation?

Everyone from my generation knows the effects of inflation simply by living through six decades. I remember that in 1966 my parents bought a brand new four bedroom home, 2 ½ baths with a two car garage for $18,000. The cost of gasoline in the early seventies was about 50 cents per gallon. In 1974 I bought a brand new V8 Chevy Camaro right out of the showroom for $4,800. This is why every baby boomer knows that the cost of things have increased drastically – the cost of living continues to go up, while the value of the dollar continues to go down.

Consider The Cost.

It is not wise to have large sums of cash in a bank account or in any financial vehicle earning less than 2% interest. Here is why, banks are paying less than 1% interest while inflation is at 2%. That means that your money is decreasing by 1% every year. In addition to that fact, the volatility of the stock market can diminish your savings greatly in one day! That is why many investors have purchased gold – it is a good hedge against inflation. Typically, when the stock market goes down, the value of gold goes up. In 1989 the value of gold was $363 per ounce – by 2011 the price had risen to $1,864 per ounce. It has not dropped below $1,000 since 2009. Currency has the potential of becoming worthless, but gold will always have value. However, before you purchase gold you really need to do your homework. I prefer the one ounce Golden Eagle coins. The consideration of these financial realities may cause you to consider converting 10% of your investments into physical gold.

Then There Is Real Estate.

If I could turn back the hand of time, I would invest every penny in real estate. When you compare real estate to any other investment, it makes the most sense with the least amount of risk. Let me qualify that statement with an actual example; Three years ago I transferred $45,000 from my IRA account to my self-directed IRA because the returns were low. I also purchased a *fixer up* townhouse for rental purposes.

The costs associated with this venture were: $45,000 Purchase Price, $2,000 for Closing, and $12,000 for Renovation cost. Remember, in order to ascertain whether this was a sound investment, one needs to calculate the ROI (Return On Investment). The following is pertinent:

Annual Rent: $1,200 X 12 = $14,400

Home Owner Association Fees (HOA): $70 X 12 = $840

Taxes per Quarter: $1,000 X 4 = $4,000

Annual Management Fees: $120 X 12 = $1,400

ROI Calculations Continued:

Total Investment Costs: $45,000 (Purchase Price) + $2,000 (Closing Costs) + $12,000 (Renovation) = $68,000

$$ROI = \frac{14,400 - (\$840 + \$4,000 + \$1,400)}{\$68,000} \times 100 = 12\%$$

That $45,000 which previously sat in an account earning less than 5%, has now earned me a steady 12% for the last three years.

Decisions.

The results mentioned above have enabled me to make wise decisions. Over the last 4 years I liquidated all my stocks and bought rental properties. I no longer have to worry about the volatility of the markets. The stock market in its best bull run era could never sustain an annual average of 12%. Note, I am not talking against the market, instead I view it as a means toward a better end!

There are a lot of real estate gurus out there selling their programs for thousands of dollars. However, you can obtain the same education by joining your local REIA (Real Estate Investors' Association). They are located all over the United States with the cost of membership being as little as $150 per year.

CHAPTER 5

BUILDING WEALTH

The Concept of Wealth.

Wealth is a relative term – the poorest in some nations would be considered wealthy in another. Generally speaking, wealth means having abundance. The goal of this book is to show the reader how to create sustainable wealth.

Jobs As a Wealth Builder.

There are four basic ways that people try to accumulate wealth. The most common method is through a job. When I was hired thirty three years ago, we were told, "You'll never get rich working here, but you will make a good living." They were absolutely right – that's true of most jobs, regardless of how much you make.

I recall a fellow employee boasting about working so much overtime that he doubled his regular salary. There was so much overtime for so many years that the availability was taken for granted. But there came a time when the hours were drastically reduced, and many individuals struggled to live off of their regular pay. What really happened here? Well, some people failed to realize that overtime is not a guarantee and you should not live dependent upon it! In addition it puts one in a higher tax bracket.

Many of the employees took their jobs for granted because the company never had a layoff in the history of the plant. Eventually however, the plant became fully automated, making some tasks redundant, and even eliminated some jobs. This forced many employees to accept lower paying positions. I learned through discussions with several co-workers that they were fearful of retirement. This fear was based on their belief that their pay at retirement would not be enough to sustain their lifestyle.

A job is not a realistic vehicle for building wealth. No matter how much people earn, their cost of living is usually close to their income. That makes a job, in itself, a poor method for building wealth.

Sole proprietor as a wealth building vehicle.

There are those who choose sole proprietorship as their wealth building vehicle. These are fearless and highly motivated individuals who prefer working for themselves. However, one should know that there are both advantages and disadvantages to being your own boss.

Advantages vs. disadvantages of sole proprietorship.

Some of the advantages that may fuel an individual's decision to be a sole proprietor are: they receive 100% of the profit, they determine their work schedule, and the number of hours to dedicate to the business, as well as when they should retire. It should be noted however, that with all of that freedom comes much responsibility. They are responsible for 100% of their healthcare insurance, they are the sole contributor to their IRA and life insurance. Additionally, they do not receive paid sick or vacation days – if they don't work, they don't get paid.

Considering The Cost.

I know some sole proprietors, and they usually make in one day what the average person would make in a week. It would appear that such a person would eventually become wealthy. The truth of the matter is that it's rare for a self-employed person to become wealthy. Remember, profit is what's left after all expenses are paid. There's an old saying, "It costs to be the boss!" Consider their cost for individual healthcare, life insurance, supplies, equipment, licensing, IRA contributions, and taxes, etc., then add their cost of living expenses to gain a proper picture. You will discover that the self-employed person is just living a little better than those working at a job. Additionally, they typically work more hours, and retire later. The quality of their retirement years will depend on how much they saved in their IRA and Social Security.

The Business Owner.

The third avenue that a few people choose toward wealth building is to engage a business enterprise. Such individuals are highly motivated. Their difference when compared with others is that they are usually visionaries who look beyond their own personal abilities – they know how to leverage themselves through others and the Internet. The advent of the Internet saw traditional businesses diminishing. It has greatly reduced the need for the use of a brick & mortar building as a dedicated office. This means that the usual overhead cost such as rent, utilities, insurance and employee costs are greatly reduced. This is the pathway of many multi-level marketing businesses.

Leveraging and Motivation.

The business owner who uses the principle of leveraging often has an online store for their product or services. They increase their sales by recruiting highly motivated individuals like themselves who also desire to create wealth. This is leveraging yourself – ten people working together can accomplish far more with less effort than one person could.

Over the years I have met some wealthy individuals with thousands of people in their organization. Whenever I attended three day international conventions, and listened to the inspiring testimonies of how some of them overcame poverty and adversities, I would wonder, "What's my problem?" I realized after much soul searching that I did not wish my success to depend on keeping others motivated. This then led me to question the sustainability of the wealth gained by such people.

These types of businesses can experience a domino effect when there are a few defectors from the enterprise. Just like the others, it will require your constant attention and effort to maintain the same level of income. In my opinion, it still sounds like a job. My explanation of the fourth way to build wealth will explain why I have this conviction.

Investing – A Sound Way to Build Wealth.

The fourth and last way some people try to build wealth is by investing. It is the road least traveled, yet it's the most efficient. Unlike the other methods, it does not require your constant effort to maintain the wealth you build initially. It will not rely on an organization of human efforts to leverage your investments. I can tell you from the experience gained while working a job for 30 years, owning a karate studio for 7 years, and being a home remodeling contractor for 20 years as well as being an investor for 6 years, that Investing is the best way to build wealth. The other methods can serve as a means toward an end.

The Challenge.

The biggest challenge with investing is the need to overcome fear. Most people associate investing with high risk. That's true, depending on the investment. I choose real estate, more specifically rentals, because of its stability and high returns. People are familiar with flipping shows. It is true that you can make big returns in a short period of time. However, you have to keep doing it in order to keep the money flowing. Once again, that sounds too much like a job. On the other hand, should you invest in fixing up a rental, then hire a management company for 10% to find, screen potential tenants, and to collect the rent, you would avoid many pitfalls if done correctly – you would not experience some of the nightmares you may have heard from some landlords.

Possible Sources for Funds to Invest.

The reason rental investment is a great source for sustainable wealth, lies in the fact that, regardless of whether you work or not, rental investments will continue to produce a steady source of income for you.

The next challenge to the desire to invest is finding the necessary funds. Simply put, where do you get the money? Let me list a few resources, with some obviously better than others; home equity loans, hard money lenders, private lenders, banks, and the self-directed IRA are just a few. It would be a wise observation that the least tapped resource, yet the most beneficial, is the self-directed IRA. The beauty of this strategy is that all of the income generated is tax deferred. That means that you could have one million dollars in rental income each year, and only be taxed on the amount you withdraw in a given year. There are three essentials that people will always need, food, clothing, and rentals!

>> CHAPTER 6 <<

GOD'S FAVOR

The Basis of It All.

Proverbs 3:5-6 (NKJV) says, *"Trust in the Lord with all your heart and lean not on your own understanding; in all your ways acknowledge Him, and he shall direct your paths."* This is the last chapter of this presentation and I want to end this book the way I began it. It is important that you understand that all the financial knowledge in the world means nothing without God's favor. When I retired I realized that unless I leveraged my IRA savings, there was a possibility that I might outlive my money. So, I got down on my knees and prayed this prayer, *"Lord, I am depending on you for wisdom and favor. This is Your money and I will honor You with its increase."* That was a sincere request and vow I made to God. Although I knew somethings, I was persuaded that my Heavenly Father knows far more and can see what I am unable to see.

The Benefits of God's Wisdom and Favor.

We can avoid so many mistakes when we seek His counsel. I needed His wisdom to make the right decisions. Wisdom is the ability to use knowledge properly. I will take God's favor over anything because He can administer His favor in an unfavorable situation and use it to my advantage.

Some Testimonies.

Allow me to share some personal testimonies that will establish this truth concerning God's favor. I remember one year when my goal was to purchase two condos but, I only had funds to buy one while retaining a balance of $35,000 in my account. At that time, no one was selling below $50,000. I prayed about it and then offered $45,000 to one owner and $40,000 to the other – both offers were accepted! In case that didn't excite you, listen to this next testimony. One year later, although I put multiple bids in to acquire other properties, I only had enough to purchase one at the time. My offer was accepted for a townhouse, one of two offers I made. Two days later, my offer on a ranch style home was also accepted. Now, you must understand that I was $20,000 short, and therefore considered rescinding the offer. A couple of days later, I was approached by a real estate agent while at the realty office completing the papers for the townhouse. She knew about the rancher, but nothing concerning my financial situation. She wanted to know if she could invest $20,000 for $25,000 in return. Well, you could have knocked me over with a feather. I rented that house for two years and then sold it. I discovered that my niche was townhouses. This leads me into my next testimony.

The Value of Periodic Evaluations.

This testimony begins with a reevaluation of my real estate investments. After having success with several rentals, I had a bad experience with a tenant. Although condos are low in maintenances costs and taxes, yet their HOA fees tend to be high. When I did the math, I discovered that the Townhouses yielded the best return for my investment. I decided to sell the condo vacated by the bad tenant. I then engaged a realtor to list it at only $5,000 over the purchase price, and to offer a 5 year seller financing option @ 0%, with $5,000 down.

Here is God's providence at work! My son (whose name is the same as mine), called me within two weeks of the listing mentioned above. He had received inquiries from a female he knew. She saw the listing and the owner's name from public records. My son gave her my phone number, and within a week she signed a sale agreement. In addition to a quick sale, I received favor when a listing agent declined to receive the commission which was 6% of the sale price. Her reason was that since I found a buyer in two weeks, she did not feel right in taking a commission. I thanked her, and one month later went to settlement.

Prayer and Strategy.

It dawned on me after a year of receiving monthly payments that this was a great strategy. It was highly lucrative to sell a property quickly and receive higher monthly payments without the expense and responsibility of ownership. Essentially, you are the bank in a seller financing senario. In this particular case, I offered 0%, an offer that no bank would ever entertain.

The experience persuaded me to obtain another townhouse by utilizing a similar strategy-sell a condo to obtain the necessary collateral. Since I had become a mentor to the lawyer who bought the last condo, I decided to ascertain whether she would be interested in a similar deal. She requested a week to think about it. She accepted my offer a week later.

I have learned that when you develop symbiotic relationships, you usually experience more success. I was offering the lawyer a deal she could never get by using a bank. Meanwhile, I was receiving a better return than when I was renting the property.

Now, before I forget and take the credit for those transactions, let me state that it was only after I had prayed that the relevant strategy came to my mind. Some people have a narrow view of Jesus' statement which indicated that the Holy Spirit would bring all things to our remembrance. Every time that I was faced with a business decision I would ask, "Well Lord what are we going to do now?" Time after time things that I learned in the past would come to mind. I take no credit because I did not purposely think of those things.

Let God Be The Guide.

I am reminded of my first *flip* that *flopped*. I bought my first townhouse for a good price with cash. Unfortunately I was too ambitious and spent as much money *rehabbing* as I did purchasing the property. When the house was completed and listed, I soon realized that I was in a rental market. Let me assure you, every investor will make a mistake. The question is, can he correct it? I was feeling the pressure of having invested a considerable amount of money without getting one offer. I knew that it was time for me to consult my Heavenly Father about my problem.

What About Lease Option?

The term lease option came to my mind after a few days. I knew that it was a strategy that I had learned years ago. However, I could not recall the specifics. After reviewing my text books and notes, I listed the property as a 2 year lease with the option to purchase, and with the requirement for a non-refundable deposit of $5,000. I received an offer from a young couple with a newborn within a month. Again I repeat – if you give people opportunities that no one else will, not only will it benefit them, but you as well. After they walked through the newly renovated house, they were anxious to move in. Two years later I sat down with them to discuss their options. It was their option to either buy the property or to rent. They chose the latter, and to this day they are one of my best tenants.

God's Favor – Not Luck.

When things work in their favor, some people think it's either luck or chance but, the footsteps of a righteous man are ordered by the Lord. Our church began 2019 with a challenge to believe God for what we wanted from Him. One of my requests was to acquire two more rentals for that year. I was looking and making offers from the start. But on every occasion the agents would inform me that the property was already under contract. Further, there were no townhouses available, so I pursued the acquisition of condos, but with similar results.

Now it was October, and I said to the Lord, *"I don't have enough money, and time is running out. But I know that You are the God of impossibilities!"* One Sunday that very month, I offered a ride to a new member of the church I attend. When we arrived at his apartment, I mentioned to him that I had tried to purchase in his complex on several occasions without success. He informed me that his landlord had been talking about selling over a year ago. Many of the units were going for $10,000 more than I had. However, after negotiating with the seller, I was able to purchase the unit at a price I could afford. At that point half of my initial goal for the year was accomplished, and my cash was very low. Consequently, I decided to apply for a bank loan to acquire the second condo.

Let God Do The Figuring.

One lesson that I have learned in my walk of faith is that it's not my job to figure out how God is going to accomplish what I asked Him to do. That's why He is God and we are not!

Shortly after I got the first condo under contract, I received a call from a childhood friend who lives in California. We had reconnected the previous year for the first time in almost thirty years. He was in town for his nephew's wedding who I discovered, previously lived across the street from my home. We first met at age 12 through a mutual friend. Since we were casual friends, and never kept up with each other, I was surprised to hear from him. When he flew into town for the wedding, we hung out together for a few days reminiscing about the past. I was encouraged to learn that he was a born-again Believer. We both vowed to keep in touch after the wedding.

I was not surprised to receive a call from him this time. He wanted to know the usual, "What's going on?" My response, "Nothing much, I am just waiting on the bank's decision concerning my loan request to buy some real estate." I was surprised at his next query. He asked, "If I could offer you a better rate would you consider a loan from me?" Let me interrupt this testimony for a minute to point out that, this is what I mean by God's favor. Here is an individual who has seen me just once in thirty years, a casual friend who lives in California, yet is willing to loan me $70,000 dollars @ 5% interest for 5 years.

I thank God for His favor because I would never ask nor solicit the backing of my investments by anyone, other than a financial institution. The difference here is that *he* asked me. Before I enter into any agreement I do the math – I always ensure that I am able to honor my agreement. I believe that a person's integrity is far more important than his bank account.

The advantage of being funded by a private lender is that you don't have all the red tape usually presented by a bank. In fact, as soon as I saw a good deal on the MLS (Multiple Listing Service), I immediately made a cash offer – had I waited on the bank, the property would probably have been sold. Before 2019 was over, I had my two properties. Last month when the Pandemic of 2020 was devastating the stock market, my friend sent me a text in which he stated, "I am looking at the market crash and am very pleased that we are doing business together."

I will repeat what I said at the beginning of this book. We are stewards of God's money, and if we continue to give Him a return from our investments, He will continue to fund them!

>> CONCLUSION <<

Financial planning will relieve a lot of stress in your life, and also give you a pathway toward freedom from debt. It is said that, *"The definition of insanity is doing the same thing in the same way, yet expecting a different result."* I would add to that – you need to change your thinking about tithing, spending, saving, and investing. Remember, no one cares more about your situation than you. So, you need to take charge of your finances. It's going to require faith, patience, and perseverance to be financially free. Last, but not least, you need to acknowledge the presence of God in every aspect of your life, especially in your finances.

>> PRAYER FOR SALVATION <<

The Scriptures of Romans 10:9-10 (NKJV) says *"that if you confess with your mouth the Lord Jesus, and believe in your heart that God has raised Him from the dead, you will be saved. For with the heart one believes unto righteousness, and with the mouth confession is made unto salvation."* Heavenly Father, I believe in my heart that God raised Jesus from the dead, and I now confess that with my mouth – I accept Jesus as my Lord and Savior. I am now reborn, I am a Christian. Now Lord, I am asking you to fill me with the Holy Spirit. I receive Him now in Jesus' name. Amen.

Printed in the United States
By Bookmasters